THE RING OF LIFE: STILL STANDING

Author Charlotte Denise Hill

Table of Contents

DEDICATION

This book is in honor and memory of my dear mother, the late Betty Irene Cox Williams (Betty Bop). You were such a beautiful soul. Your outer beauty was equal to your inner beauty. It was such an honor to be your daughter.

To my eldest sister Venus V. Green, thank you from the depths of my soul for sharing your story with me and filling in the gaps. I didn't know some of the abuse you endured and how you had to cope with the scars throughout the years. You were abused from the age of nine until you were sixteen. You protected us younger kids even when we didn't know you were doing it. I will forever be grateful for your selfless acts. Big sis, you will always be my protector and one of my heroes. I love you for life.

To my sister Tina T. Williams, thank you for being my strong prayer warrior. You evolved into such a powerhouse amid our trials. I recall you trying to take your life. I didn't know at the time that you were trying to escape your personal hell. Tippy had done horrible things to you also. You suffered in silence. You hid your internal pain well, but God knew. He saw. He refused to let you die. Thank you for not losing your faith. I love you to the moon and back.

To my brother Elder Will Williams Jr., I thank GOD for the man you have become. Even when we were younger, you were the real man of the house. As the eldest brother, you shielded me from so many dangers. You placed yourself in harm's way for your family. I was also clueless about the pain and humiliation you battled as a young man. I can only say that I am proud to have you as a brother. GOD has showered you with the blessings of Abraham, and you deserve every one of them. I love you with the love of God. Continue to allow the Lord to use you and change the lives of so many in the process. I love

1

you (BB).

To my sister Claudia C. Bell, my brother Tamar D. Williams, and Deandre E. Williams, you all were too young to know what was happening in our home. All of us older siblings did our best to shield and protect you from anything or anyone that could have harmed you. You all were deeply loved and still are. I love each of you dearly.

Thanks to my children Andrea, Mark, and my twins Lorraine and Fredrick for loving me, flaws and all. I wasn't the best mom, yet you understood and stood by me. I love you guys so much. I struggled through the years fighting demons in my head that hunted and tormented me. To terminate my mental anguish, I tried killing myself. Yet, you never left my side. To my eldest daughter Andrea, thank you for my beautiful grandchildren, DaJa, Keyedrick, and Keya. Thank you to my granddaughter DaJa for giving me three beautiful and gifted great-grandbabies, twins Christian and Christopher, and my little princess Charidy.

Thanks, Fredrick, for giving me my twin Monet (MOMO). Thank you, Lorraine and Jarvis, for giving me my miracle baby Julianna (Duda Bear). Now it's your turn Mark (smile). I'm waiting for my grandbaby. I am thankful to God for allowing me to be a part of my children's lives, my grandchildren's, and my great-grandchildren's. Thank you, JESUS!

Honorary Mentions

I thank the Late Elder James Madison Johnson and Lady Beverly Johnson (Bailey Temple COGIC) for treating us like we were your own. I will always love you for showing us the Love of God in action. Elder Randall L. Greenwood and Missionary Roxanna Greenwood (Bailey Temple COGIC), I thank each of you for caring enough to feed my children and me when I didn't have the resources to do so. My heart will always beat with love and gratitude toward you.

Thanks to missionary Dollie Bennet Milfort (Bailey Temple C.O.G.I.C) for praying for my children and me and always being there with a listening ear. I love you to life. May God's blessings be upon you. Sister Lynn Reece, my sister from another mother, I love you also.

Sister Tamatha Wilson, you're also my sister from another mother. You have cried with me, laughed with me, and stuck by my side. True friends are rare. However, I can say that you are a friend indeed. I love you with the love of GOD. You are my prayer partner, my text buddy, and my ride and live sister (smile). Know that you are loved and that there is no other like you.

James G. Williams, you are my BFF for life, my brother, cousin, and friend. You have been with me through thick and thin. I love you more than you could ever know. You and your mother were always there when my children and I were homeless and everything else we battled. You were there to give us a place to call home. You and your mom are a blessing from GOD. I love you both so very much.

Most importantly, God, my savior, I love you, and thank you. You are the author and finisher of my faith. Without you, this book would have never come to fruition. You gave me the courage, wisdom, strength, and knowledge to tear down the strongholds that had bound me.

Letter to Mom,

Although you are no longer here in bodily form, I know that your spirit is resting in heaven. You will always be my "Betty Boo," and I will continue to cherish your memories in my heart. It is difficult to come to terms with how much abuse you endured by the man who was supposed to love you and your children. Yet instead, for years, he abused you. My mind is stained forever with the memories of him beating you, spitting in your face, kicking you down the stairs, degrading you in front of family and friends, and giving you busted lips and blackened eyes. Although he tried to destroy you numerous times, you continued to survive. I am the woman I am today because of you. You showed the rest of us what a powerful, undefeated, strong, and courageous black woman you were. You are the epitome of a strong black woman. I applaud you for that. Mother, you didn't let the fact that you had seven children hold you back. You amazed all of us every day with your strength. Watching you conquer amazing feats only increased our love for you.

Those who claimed to be your friends abandoned you when you needed them the most. Their failure to come through didn't stop you from being loving. Despite everything, you continued to rise and shine. You wanted nothing but the absolute best for your kids. Through it all, you never gave up hope for a better life for us. For so many years, I carried enough pain for both of us. God is yet walking me through the healing process. Even now, I find myself weeping because of all that you have suffered. I miss you so much, mom.

As children, we were too young to understand the deep secrets that you kept bottled inside. You were dealing with your demons, but thankfully, GOD pulled you out of the dark, murky hole you were sinking in. Some looked at you as a fool for staying. For years I did too.

4

I blamed you for all the abuse that we experienced at the hands of Tippy. Later in life, I realized that he had enslaved you. His threats frightened you into staying. No doubt, there must've been times that you felt like you failed us, but I can assure you that you didn't. You did what you had to do to survive. I could never blame you for that. You were being coerced and held captive against your will by that old hedonistic devil incarnate.

Your mind refused to let you go free out of fear of what he would do to us. Like your false accusers, I didn't understand then fear can cause people to freeze, paralyzing them from acting. It affects people differently. Those same people never walked in your shoes nor witnessed the horrendous atrocities that you did. They didn't hear the gnarly threats that Tippy hurled at you every chance he could. I was so caught up in my feelings then that I didn't understand how devastated you must've felt as a mother to have been demoralized in front of your children and witnessed their abuse. There's no doubt in my mind that you felt powerless.

Your story is my story–all of our stories, mom. I understand now that sometimes it's not easy to leave and walk away, especially when involved with a psychopathic monster. Your children witnessed your mental and physical abuse. It became our normalcy. We, too, have been traumatized by Tippy. Every time I heard you cry for days and nights continuously, it shattered my young heart. Even now, it's hard to wrap my mind around why no one tried to rescue us, not even the pastor of the dusty, old church that sat piously erect across the street from our home. His only words of consolation were, "Pray about it." At the time, I wanted to make him swallow those words. Religious rhetoric is often a covert way for someone to avoid responsibility. Through it all, God was your rock. I watched Him pull you through the unthinkable. As he carried you, you were able to carry us out too. After years of watching,

I finally grasped the meaning of "enough is enough."

All of us children have battled with our self-esteem and had other psychological issues because of our nightmarish childhood. God placed us exactly where he wanted us to be. That was our journey. II Timothy 2: 12 says, "If we suffer, we shall also reign with him...." One day each of us will reign with Christ because of enduring the unthinkable and coming out with our faith yet intact. As for me personally, I didn't know it then, but I know it now. GOD was preparing me for my purpose. The crushing pain I experienced over the years released the oil of God's anointing over my life. Everyone has a cross to bear. There's no crown without a cross. My journey toward Golgotha was a long and tedious one. Looking back, I am grateful that we remained faithful to each other.

Despite all the hell that Venus, Tina, Will, Claudia, Tamar, Deandre, and I have suffered, it is incredible how close we all have become. Our bond is unbreakable. You would be so proud. Each of us has become so strong. So many families fall apart and never recover from such abuse, but we did. It is our powerful testimony. They all spoil me rotten and shower me with lots of love and affection. I love them all more than they know. Each of them means the world to me.

Mommy, thank you from the depths of my heart and soul for being my rock, shelter, friend, and comfort. I love and miss you so much; words cannot explain how much you meant to me. I miss talking with you, eating your food, and watching old western movies together. Amusingly, I am becoming more and more like you every day. I even find myself watching the same movies you liked and eating foods I thought I would never eat. That would tickle you. I wish that I could have taken all of your sufferings away. Regardless, you are resting with God now. For that, I am grateful. You are finally at peace.

Please forgive me for any wounds I may have added to the damage. From the deepest parts of my heart, I apologize. I am so sorry. Please forgive me, mom.

Sincerely,

Charlotte

INTRODUCTION

First, I will start by saying that many parents try to conceal things from their children, but I am a witness that they can usually sense when energy shifts occur. They might be too young to understand what is happening around them, but from my experience, they know something isn't right. Often a child blames him or herself for the disharmony in the home and labels themself as bad. Many behavioral changes occur when they feel the energy shift but can't interpret it. It was my truth.

The enemy often uses soul wounds early in a child's life to distort their identity. If not uprooted, they will eventually become a stronghold in the person's adult life. It will become the threshing floor, the place in the individual's life where he will self-sabotage and derail their life repetitively. It will become a place where they must wage war with themselves and wrestle until they break free from the mental bondage of faulty beliefs and perceptions that fractures the soul.

Because trauma started early in my life, my self-image was marred. I looked at the world around me from these dark-colored lenses. Everything seemed bleak and hopeless. I hated who I was. I didn't feel like I belonged anywhere. I was just an empty shell of a person wasting away. I was a nobody headed nowhere fast. Constantly the devil prompted me to give up and throw in the towel. He tried to convince me that I would be better off dead. No matter how many times I tried to carry out his wish, the Lord blocked it and said,

"Not so. Not yet."

In life, we sometimes hide from our past misfortunes, mistakes, judgments, embarrassments, and even past hurts. Hiding and pretending became my new normalcy. Day by day, week by week, month by month, and year by year, I wore a mask and lived a lie. I ran from God and my truth because of fear of the unknown. I also suffered from a lack of understanding, a lack of knowledge, and false teachings.

I have struggled for many years with the agonizing nightmares of my past. I have some dark truths that are not easy to share. My life has so many colorful narratives–most of which I am ashamed to admit. Each thread of my story-physical and sexual abuse, homelessness, and suicidal tendencies-makes up my dramatic life. What I did is not the same as who I am. Truthfully, there are many things that I could have walked away from and perhaps avoided mishaps, but for the most part, I didn't. Nevertheless, I endured them all because I believed they were my fate.

I grew weary of my skeletons. They weighed me down. I reached a point where I wanted freedom no matter what price I had to pay. I decided to break the chains of mediocrity, soar my wings, and evolve into God's image of me. It was time to let go of the self-image that trauma molded of me. I turned to writing; it became my way of escape.

"I must write," my inner man screamed. "People need to know what has happened! They need to know about the demons I battle! They need to know the miserable condition of a broken heart and a stressful mind. They need to know why people like me choose suicide over life."

Initially, I only wrote to journal my experiences and to get the thoughts out of my head and onto paper. I eventually began toying with the idea that I could use my notes to write a book. Like the children of Israel who wandered around the wilderness for forty years, I looped around the decision to write a book and share it with the world or not. The fear of people judging me because of my past mistakes made me reconsider exposing my skeletons. What I've done and the people I've done them with would come to light. I feared that I would never be able to show my face again.

I often questioned, "Is my story worth telling? Did the world need to know what I had suffered in life? Would people judge me because of my past? Would the community accept me with all my truths? Would those at church treat me differently?" I was in a battle between my soul, heart, and mind.

After countless sleepless nights, I decided to share my story with the world. I knew it would be painful to dig up old memories. Doing so would force me to discard my mask and the pretentious attitude that "all was well" in Charlotteville. It would allow people to see the real me, raw–flaws and all.

When I first sat at the table, with pen in hand, countless thoughts raced through my mind. I fought through anyway and wrote the first sentence. It sparked a fire of courage, awakening a tenacity I didn't know I had.

Although countless self-help books and healing therapies are available, it can be difficult to erase the years of hardship and horrors from one's life. Personally, writing and reading the Word of God has been the best therapy ever. My faith in God has also given me the necessary encouragement to share my story. Each helped me to acknowledge and embrace every aspect of my life. I began to realize that every dark event in my life added contrast to my story and helped to strengthen me from within. I cried unto God, and He heard me. He powerfully came to my defense. He rescued me from the dark pit of my internal flames of anger, frustration, and fear. He became my balm in Gilead. He became the salve that allowed me to see the beauty that I possess both physically and spiritually.

I am grateful for my sisters and brothers who have supported me through this process of sharing our stories. We have been through so much together. There are no words that can express the love I have for every one of them. It was difficult reliving all of the horrible memories we all went through with Tippy, our stepfather. Trying to process them has caused a lot of shameful and hurtful emotions to resurface while writing this book.

I have concluded that we all have stories that can help someone and lead them to freedom in one area of their lives or another. My trust in God has given me boldness. Now, I am not afraid of people's responses.

This book is my attempt to bare my soul and free my spirit. It will highlight my journey from bondage to freedom. It is my way of letting people know that they are not alone. God is always there to help, heal, and guide them to survive and thrive. That is enough reason to declare my story aloud to the world. I am a witness that God can reach down in the dumps and turn a complete mess into a powerful message. He can turn horrible tests into testimonies and trials into triumphs.

This book is part of my therapeutic journey. It has allowed me to dive into the scary and dark corridors of my subconscious mind where the secrets lie and blow the dust from them. It is my way of facing my shadows and integrating them so that I may walk in wholeness and completion. Deliverance looks different for everyone. Mine happens to look and feel like a boxing match. I had plenty of breakdowns and breakthroughs along the way. Yet I keep getting back up in the ring every time I get knocked down. Just as it seems the game is over, God breathes through me and gives me my fight back. This book is my pathway to victory. It is my path to freedom in Christ.

It is evident today that God had saved me "For Such a Time As This." He spared my life to help others who are broken, downtrodden, crushed, and bruised. It is my testimony that those who are at rock bottom will listen to and find hope. May they receive enough light to see God in the middle of their trials, to help them to hang on a bit longer, and to press past their breaking points.

Without God, there would not be a Charlotte. I am thankful that He has saved me and increased grace and mercy upon my life. He has given me the courage to push past my pain and begin the healing process. He has empowered me to walk in my calling. God has provided me with an opportunity to heal by sharing my story with the world. He has empowered my soul to serve humanity and help relieve others' pain. God has given me the responsibility to help those facing the same issue I faced as a child and an adult.

Today, I am thankful God spared my life despite my suicide attempts. I am grateful because I have obtained salvation. I know that God loves me; I experience His love daily. He is my advocate. The Lord is a very present help in times of trouble. It humbles me that He did not allow me to die in my sins. He picked me up when I was down and set my life on the right course. I now serve God and have fellowship with Him. He is my comforter and strong tower. He has proven faithful and never leaves my side. He also sticks by me closer than a brother. He is my hope when I'm lonely. He walks and talks with me even during my darkest hours. His Holy Spirit, the comforter, strengthens my inner man and helps when the healing process becomes unbearable.

He is my high priest that feels my infirmities. God kept me when I couldn't manage myself. When I was a wretched mess, He covered me until I could get my life together. Every day, God reminds me of who I am. He is the only one I can call on, no matter the time. Although people may fail to honor their promises, God is always there. Isaiah

59:19 says, "When the enemy shall come in like a flood, the Spirit of the LORD shall lift a standard against him."

Because I dared to face my shadows, God has thawed my heart so that I could find true love. I didn't allow my past to cause me to run away from it. God's grace has taught me what true love is. When I saw it in the man that asked me to marry him, I knew that he was the one that God had ordained for me. On the other side of the pain, your blessing and breakthrough are waiting for you also. Don't you dare forfeit the game by quitting too soon!

As you read this book, I pray that God will reach you were ever you are. I pray that your heart will be open to receive the words that the Holy Spirit will speak to you and provide direction and instruction. God spared my life so that I might reach you. I don't take my calling lightly. You are part of my assignment. I have answered the call and will fulfill the mission through Christ, which strengthens me. The scriptures below are now the torchbearers of my life:

"2 Timothy 4:6-8 {For I am now ready to be offered, and the time of my departure is at hand. I have fought a good fight; I have finished my course, I have kept the faith; Henceforth there is laid up for me a crown of righteousness, which the Lord, the righteous judge, shall give me at the day; and not to me only, but unto all them also that love his appearing."

ROUND ONE:
No Green Grass Here

I was born on August 9, 1965. The city was Fort Myers, Florida. I was my mother's fourth child. Before giving birth to me, my mom had a little girl. Unfortunately, she passed away. She would have been one year younger than me if she had lived. Mom would later have a total of seven children. For so long, I viewed my birth as a tragedy. I wondered why I was born into a world of so much misery and pain. I cursed the day that the doctors came to my mom and said,

"It's a girl,"

She, in turn, said,

"Her name is Charlotte."

It was at this moment that my story started. Life didn't become hellish until a few years later. Yet a looming feeling that evil was always lurking near me was prevalent.

Mom and dad got married while they were young. She was only 16 at the time. They had typical marital spats, some uglier than others. They loved each other, and I know they loved us. It was difficult for them to make it as a married couple. Unfortunately, I guess mom got tired of bickering. She met another man named Ponce Deleon Jones and eventually left our dad. He had us call him by his nickname, Tippy. He promised her the moon and stars. She believed him. In addition, he treated us, her kids, well. What more could a parent ask of a potential partner? He lavished her and us with presents and told us repeatedly how much he loved us. His words and actions convinced us that he adored my mother and us kids. He often gave my siblings and me warm, long hugs. His embrace seemed genuine enough. It was a wonderful experience to feel wanted and loved by Tippy even though we were not his biological children.

At the time, Tippy was undoubtedly more seductive than Daddy. He portrayed himself as a gentleman to the fullest. The grass seemed greener on this side than on the side where mom and dad bickered a lot. However, little did mom know that sociopathic tendencies lay beneath his heroic persona. As the saying goes, things are not always what they seem. Skeletons are bound to come out sooner or later. In our case, they would manifest sooner than we could've imagined.

Mom and dad never divorced. They both said they would never remarry. Both kept that promise their entire lives. Months after mom and dad separated, Tippy moved in. It didn't take long for him to persuade her that we all needed a fresh start and would be better off moving. To keep her new love happy, mom agreed. We packed all our belongings, loaded up the vehicle, and were on our way to our land flowing with milk and honey. We were leaving behind Fort Myers, Florida and our relatives. My eldest sister Venus and I were only a few years apart. She was nine, and I was seven, about to turn eight. Because of the close age gap, we were referred to as "stair steps" by our parents.

After driving north for hours, I noticed a sign that read: "Welcome to Michigan." A few miles later, another sign read "Detroit" with "Motor City" written underneath. Excitement filled the air. A new chapter in our lives had begun. We were all anxious to see what awaited us. It was dusk when we arrived at our final destination.

Days passed. We settled into our new home and got enrolled in school. It didn't take mom and us long to start making friends and blending in. Florida soon became a distant memory. Yet, a tinge of sorrow remained because I deeply missed dad. Nothing would be able to fill the hole that only he could fill, not even all the gifts that Tippy bought us.

During our first winter, we encountered a snowstorm. Schools closed for two weeks. The experience was the best time of my life. My siblings and I had lots of fun playing in the snow with our friends and neighbors. We were living the Riley dream. We seemed like the perfect little family. Most families could only wish for the fun and love we shared.

Unfortunately, that illusion was short-lived. Tippy slowly started changing. Little things began pissing him off. I chalked it up to work-related stress. Venus and Tina were not allowed to date nor invite company over to the house, especially boys. Eventually, we were all banned from having friends over. He didn't stop there. He forbade any of us to leave the house without his permission. Our illusory happiness began to unravel quickly after that. I couldn't understand the sudden changes. I could tell that my mother was just as confused as we were. I hoped and prayed that it was only a phase he was going through.

Mom's smile started fading. Her eyes started getting sadder. She was no longer the cheerful lady she had once been. My eldest brother constantly seemed to be in a foul mood too. My eldest sister Venus became a shell of a person. She started changing right before my eyes. She used to be a social butterfly with many friends, but now, she seldom ever left the house. I was baffled. I could see the pain in her eyes, the anger in her face, and hear the embarrassment in her voice, but I had no clue what was the source of all their sudden changes.

Whenever mom was not around, Venus was the one who took care of us and protected us while we were ill. It seemed my defender, the one I could turn to for support and solace when I needed it, had begun to deteriorate. It did not matter how young I was at the time; I needed my protector. I was going to learn where she had vanished and hopefully bring her back.

My second oldest sister Tina was in the same boat, refusing to make eye contact when my mother spoke to them. Something had flipped our planet on its axis. Our world was slowly spinning out of control, and I had no clue what was causing it.

As the years wore on, our family moved from one apartment to the next.

"Why do we keep moving so much?" I questioned mom one day.

"We need a bigger place," was her only explanation.

Initially, I accepted it as truth, but the more we moved, I knew that there was another reason. There had to be. Although I was only seven, the frequent moves began to trouble me. I got tired of leaving my friends behind, starting over, and trying to make new ones. It made me feel empty inside. My young mind knew more than what my parents thought I did. I couldn't put it into words, but I understood something wasn't right. The energy of the house was drastically different than before.

What came next only reinforced that everything was not well in our home. I soon learned the truth behind the frequent relocations. Tippy started beating mom. I'm not sure if the beatings were happening prior, and he had been concealing them from us. The fact was, Tippy wasn't hiding them now. He didn't care that we witnessed him transforming into a monster before our little eyes. It was surreal. He had promised not to harm us. Yet, he often beat her so severely that she couldn't leave the house for weeks at a time. It was becoming increasingly clear that he had lied to mom. His words of endearment were nothing more than fluff. The beatings continued and worsened.

My sisters, brother, and I often huddled in a corner, crying and terrified, unable to do anything to stop him as he beat her to a pulp. He constantly stated that if any of us disclosed what he was doing, he would murder us all. We believed him. It turns out the grass wasn't green after all. It only appeared to be that way. Mom probably would've been better off sticking things out with dad.

At the time, we were living in a three-bedroom apartment. Another family was staying in the upper flat above ours. During the nights and days when Tippy beat mom, I knew they had to hear what was happening in our house. Yet, no one ever showed up to assist us or call the police. Instead, they acted like they were afraid to say anything to us. They avoided us like the plague. It was mind-boggling that people could be cruel and not help when obviously, we were in danger. The least they could've done was call the police, but instead, they chose to do nothing.

ROUND TWO:
Face to Face with the Devil

By the time I turned nine, birthdays no longer held any significance. I had the same wish yearly, for mom to leave Tippy. She didn't. In 1975, mom discovered she was pregnant. I was livid.

"How could you have a baby with this monster after everything he has done to you?"

Inwardly, every fiber of my being shrieked in accusation at her. I knew that our lives would become a living nightmare now. Each child with Tippy would only make it harder to escape his control. I was almost relieved for my deceased older sister. At least she didn't have to witness or undergo the atrocities caused by Tippy. Although we didn't talk about her much, I knew mom missed her dearly. I often wondered about her personality.

After my younger brother was born in August of that year, the beatings subsided briefly. Everything appeared to be returning to normal. Tippy treated us better than usual. Yet, the look of regret and humiliation was evident in everyone's eyes. They continued to walk on eggshells. I was still curious about what stole the beam from Venus and Tina's eyes, causing their heads to drop in despair and shame. I wouldn't stop until I found out.

We relocated again by the time my mother became pregnant in 1976. She went into labor on November 15th of that same year. While in the hospital, my brother and I conspired together, agreeing that we would write down everything that happened in the house while she was away. We would give her our notes when she returned. I hoped to finally discover why my sisters were so depressed and constantly moped around the house.

My ears and eyes were wide open. I didn't want to miss any details in my daily records. I had to be sure everything I recorded was accurate to avoid misunderstandings.

When Tippy returned from the hospital, he informed us that our mom had given birth to another boy. We were joyful and terrified at the same time. Usually, I had never been concerned about staying alone with him before. However, I was this time.

The night started as usual, but around 8 p.m., Tippy asked us to go to our rooms. I jotted this information down on my notepad. At this time, Will, Claudia, and I shared a room. Venus, Tina, and Tamar shared one.

A few hours before midnight, I awakened to a presence standing by my bed. It was Tippy. I pretended to be asleep. Tippy watched my younger sister and me for a few minutes, turned, and left the room. I leaped from the bed and peered through the cracked door. He walked straight towards the bedroom where my eldest siblings were. Minutes later, he exited the room with Venus following behind him. They entered mom and his bedroom. The door shut behind them.

"Aha!" I whispered, suddenly realizing why my sisters had changed so dramatically. Tears streamed down my face as I crumpled to the floor in a heap. Only God knew what that sick bastard was doing to them. What I saw explained why they constantly looked depressed. I didn't know what to do or who to tell. I picked up my pen and paper and wrote what I observed.

I stayed up the remainder of the night worrying about Venus, wondering what he was doing to her and how I could save her. Around 5:30 am, Tippy's bedroom door opened, and Venus exited. Her eyes blazed with fury and pain. I was speechless.

"Is there anything I can say to reassure her? Should I tell her I knew what Tippy was up to and that I was documenting everything while mom was in the hospital? Would it be better if I kept my mouth shut?" I didn't have a clue what I should do under the circumstances.

Tippy left the house later that day. We were all awake by then. I kept my mouth shut about what I had witnessed. While away, he bought all of us gifts. He gave Venus more than the rest of us. I guess as a way of hushing her up. I had no interest in the psycho or anything he had to offer. I saw straight through his gimmicks. In my opinion, he was despicable. Nothing could compel me to have any sympathy or affection for him again. He was the enemy. I had to get rid of him, no matter the cost.

The following night, he took Tina to the bedroom he and our mom shared. Like Venus, he released her in the wee hours of the morning. For the remaining nights, while my mom was away, he took turns alternating between them both. Like a top spy, I continued to jot down everything.

The day before mother was to return, Will and I compared notes with one another and debated whether we should share them with her when she came home. We knew that there was a possibility that she wouldn't believe us, or worse, she would blame Venus and Tina for being hot in the tail. We decided to show her the notes anyway. I prepared myself mentally and emotionally. I accepted my fate, whatever it would be.

When she returned home, Will and I disclosed the truth about her beloved Tippy, who claimed he loved her and her children. We gave her our notes. To our dismay, she began to weep while reading over them. Suddenly she started yelling for Tippy to come here. As he did, she began shouting at him.

"How could you put your filthy hands on my kids?!" She screamed.

"I don't know what you're talking about," he lied, looking as if he had a soul and a conscience.

"Yes, you do. It's all right here," mom said, shoving our scribbled notes into Tippy's chest. It had outlined his every move.

His eyes began sweeping over the letter rapidly.

"This is bullshit," he said as a look of anger washed over his face. "Who gave you these lies?"

" We did," Will and I both confessed.

"They don't have any reason to lie," mom said, quickly defending us.

Without another word, Tippy stormed out of the room. Minutes later, he returned. Mother's eyes widened before screaming hysterically. Our gaze followed hers. Tippy was standing in the doorway holding a shotgun. He barged into the room, threatening to shoot Will and me for lying on him. Will started crying profusely.

"I did it! I did it!" I exclaimed. "Will didn't have anything to do with it!" I did not care about my safety. I was willing to endure whatever he had to dish out. My first focus was on ensuring the safety of my loved ones–especially moms. I was ready to die to protect any of them. Death would've been better than living with this monster.

Tippy walked over and rammed the gun to my head. I stared face to face with the devil. Venus and Tina began sobbing and shaking uncontrollably in the corner.

"Please don't! Stop it!" My mother begged and pleaded.

He ignored her and instead cocked the gun. I was sure I was going to die that night.

"If you ever lie on me again, I will shoot all of you motherfuckers," he said, glaring into my eyes and darting them quickly around the room.

We were all piss-scared after that.

Later that night, while waiting for sleep to come, I begged God to let me know why he didn't allow Tippy to take my life. I was whirling with questions I needed answers from Tippy as well. I wanted to ask him,

"Why would you do this to my sisters? You said you love us and wouldn't harm us, but why are you doing it now? What changed? What happened to you that caused you to turn out this way?" The only sound came from a symphony of crickets outside the window.

Days turned into weeks, months, and eventually years. Mom decided to stay with that devil after everything Will and I had disclosed to her. I was bitter and secretly resented her. It felt like she was making it alright for him to hurt us. I questioned God.

"Why have you deserted us? Why are you allowing this man to hurt your children?" Although he never answered, I developed an understanding heart. I soon realized mom was a victim herself. I could only imagine how she felt inside. She was terrified of Tippy carrying out his threats of killing us all. She knew that he was capable of doing so. Living with such a man no doubt had wreaked havoc on her self-esteem and self-worth. Every aspect of her life was under his control. She tried leaving multiple times afterward but to no avail.

When things got too crazy, mom would flee the house with the clothes we had on our backs. We would sleep at bus stops and ride buses all day. She didn't know who she could turn to, who would come to our aid. She had seven mouths to feed in addition to hers. The realization of this terrified her. Instinctively, she always took us back home when finding food became too difficult. She rationalized that at least we would have a roof over our heads and full bellies, even if it meant enduring Tippy's evil ways. She did what she felt was best at the moment. She chose to suffer. In the process, we suffered with her.

We did not speak to anyone for a few weeks after Tippy had threatened to kill Will and me with his gun, not even each other. I spent much of my time in the room alone, eating very little and wishing to disappear. To avoid hurting my family any more than they already were, I tried my best not to anger Tippy so that he wouldn't take his frustrations out on them.

Tippy started committing his atrocities away from the house after exposure to his rape and molestation. When he claimed he was going to the store or his relatives' homes, he started taking my sisters along for the ride. Tippy would drive off with one or the other and not return until hours later. He sometimes alternated between Venus and Tina. When they returned, you could see the anguish in their eyes. I could tell that they had been crying.

I wondered where they had gone and what he was making them do. Although I was young and naive, I was pretty sure it wasn't good, and I would be next, eventually.

I found out much later that he was taking them to a hotel on 14th street and prostituting them with one of his friends.

24

ROUND THREE:
The Birthday Blues

One day in 1977, while on summer break, Tina collapsed in the store while we were out shopping. Mom and Tippy rushed her to the hospital and then dropped us off. When they returned home later that day, she walked straight to her room without saying anything. Mom and Tippy were eerily quiet as well. When we questioned mom about her welfare, she stated she had acquired a virus. That was the only information provided.

Two days later, they took her back to the doctor. They were gone the entire day. I noticed the pain on my mother's face when they returned. It wasn't until much later that I found out my sister was pregnant. They forced her to have an abortion.

Venus was 14, my older brother was 12, and I was about to turn 11. By now, I had a 7-year-old sister, a 1-year-old brother, and a 2-year-old brother. I was relieved they had no idea what the family was going through. Even though they were infants, I'm sure they could still sense all of our pain.

Tina, then 13, had reached her breaking point. The same year was her first attempt to take her life. She overdosed on mother's medication. Venus also was suicidal. She used to sit on the overpass and watch cars zoom by on the freeway underneath, contemplating whether to jump or not. Both had plenty of failed attempts. I also had suicidal tendencies. I toyed with the idea of killing myself many times and have attempted to do so. Taking my life seemed like the best way out. Yet I'm still here in the land of the living.

Why wouldn't God just let me die? Why wasn't I brave enough to follow through with my plans and succeed? So many questions plagued my mind. It's obvious now that it wasn't my destiny. God wasn't finished with me because He had a purpose and plan for my life. The life-saving angel always defeated the life-taking angel, and I always survived.

The thought of God's love was so far from my mind while being abused. It's not that it wasn't available to me, but my heart was closed to it. Truthfully, I was unhappy with God, and part of me blamed Him for allowing it to happen. I was so angry that He didn't strike Tippy down. Instead, God watched as he groped my young body with filthy hands. I wondered what we had done to deserve the frequent abuse and why God didn't intervene on our behalf. There were no answers to my numerous questions.

In the years to come, I learned that Tippy had been sexually assaulting Venus and Tina while in Florida, at 8 and 9 years old. Fear of someone finding out was the real reason he moved us to Detroit. It wasn't to have a fresh start after all. Instead, it was to conceal his criminal acts. I soon realized then that he had also abused Will, who was only a year older than me. This realization only made me more afraid of him. I was frightened to do anything around Tippy–sleep, eat, or move.

By now, I had a 7-year-old sister, a 1-year-old, and a 2-year-old brother. I was relieved they had no idea what the family was going through, at least not psychologically. Venus was 14, and my older brother was 12. My 11th birthday was fast approaching. I was terrified of becoming a year older. Birthdays used to be thrilling, but now they were just another day. I especially didn't look forward to it because it meant one more year that my body was maturing. I didn't know if I would become Tippy's next victim or not; only time would tell. Little did I know, he was waiting for my period to start. In his eyes, I would then be ripe for the picking. Despite my fears, I was happy that I would be a year closer to becoming 18 so I could live on my own, get a place, and take my family away from the hellhole we called home. Then I would be better equipped to protect them.

I feared nighttime to the point where going to bed triggered anxiety within me. I could not sleep at all. I was terrified to close my eyes at night because I did not know what to expect when I reopened them. That night, like so many others, I saw Tippy slithering into my sister's room as he had done for the past year.

I kept our abuse a secret. I was afraid to tell anyone what was happening in our home. Tippy had threatened to murder the entire family multiple times if any of us talked. I could not let that happen, so I turned inwards with my thoughts.

My soul was empty. I had lost my voice. What happened to it? Would it ever be discovered again? Is it gone for good? I could only hope and pray for the best.

The end of the school year was fast approaching. Usually, this excited me, but I was more terrified than ever. It meant more time at home with Tippy.

The dreaded day finally arrived, my birthday. I was now 11 years old. I had the birthday blues. Of course, there was slight excitement, but mostly terror of what it would mean for me. Would I be the next victim of the sexual predator disguised as my mom's live-in boyfriend, or would he remain satisfied with looting my siblings' bodies and robbing them of their purity? I lay on the bed and prayed.

"Lord, who am I, and why am I here? Please cover me and protect me from all manners of evil."

As usual, there was no response. I leaped out the bed and tiptoed to the bathroom. Today should've been a day of great rejoicing and celebration, but honestly, I didn't care what my family had planned for me. All I could think about was counting down the time for bedtime. I never knew what nightfall had in store. Monsters indeed go bumpety bump in the dark. I should know; I lived with one. I splashed water on my face and then brushed my teeth. I heard some rustling in mom's and Tippy's room. I hoped and prayed I could make it through the day without drama. I finished freshening up and walked back to the room.

Later that day, I was outside playing with my siblings. I could feel Tippy eyeing me from the window. As if he knew that I was aware of what he wanted, he came to the door and opened it.

"Charlotte, come here."

I froze in my tracks; I couldn't speak. My heart pounded in my ear.

"I said come here. Now!" Tippy threatened. He then told my siblings to stay outdoors.

I immediately knew that he was up to no good.

"Your mother's gone shopping with a neighbor," he whispered as I walked past him.

He headed for the basement and motioned me to follow. The closer I got to the door, the more fear I felt in every cell of my body.

"What is he going to do to me? Is he going to carry out his earlier promise to kill me and put an end to my life for good? Should I fight or call for help? Would anyone come and rescue me if I do?" Horrid thoughts assaulted my mind as I descended the stairs.

Tippy was waiting for me at the bottom behind the door. He grabbed my arm and pulled me close to his thin body. The free hand slithered down my pants. With it, he began rubbing my vagina. The other hand stroked my breasts.

"No, stop," I said, trying to pull away.

"Hush! You better not tell your mom, not even a soul," he breathed, thrusting his fingers deeper inside my young flesh.

I felt sick to my stomach.

"You're changing into a lovely young woman," he said while rubbing and stroking my girl parts.

"Where is mom? What's taking her so long," I thought. I wondered if she knew what this pervert was doing to me.

I felt so dirty, so cheap, and so violated. All I wanted to do was scrub every inch of my body to remove Tippy's scent.

"Go back outside and play," he said after satisfying himself. Just like that, he had finished.

That day, a part of me died inside. I left that basement a different person. I took the walk of shame as I exited outdoors. It was hard acting as if nothing had just happened. I could tell by how my siblings darted their eyes from mine that they knew Tippy had just violated me. Of course, they knew all too well.

Part of me was delighted that Tippy didn't enter my room that night, but I knew what that meant. I was sickened by the thought that he was probably raping one of my sisters. Tippy had started getting mom intoxicated so that she would be knocked out for hours at a time so he could have his way with us. Venus was supposed to watch us younger siblings whenever she passed out.

For years I engraved demeaning things about me and my life on the walls and ceilings of my bedroom. I begged and pleaded for God to rescue me, save me, and for Tippy to keep his creepy hands to himself. Yet instead, my mother's eyes continued to darken with bruises, and the late-night molestations continued. I believed I was unlovable. God's silence only reaffirmed this belief. I wondered if I was created to be raped, tortured, humiliated, damaged, and misplaced? These were the few questions I had been asking myself for so long. How did I get here? And what was my ultimate goal? My mind was blank.

During these dark periods of my life, feelings of happiness and love were foreign to me. I spent many sleepless nights pacing the floor. Too afraid to sleep, I prayed for daylight while watching for any traces of light to break through the curtains. Sometimes the fear was so unbearable that severe panic attacks would wash over my body. Constantly I wondered what was wrong with me, if I was losing my mind. It was difficult for me to live with so many forces working against my life. Through experience, I came to learn that God didn't make mistakes. He always has a plan, even when we can't discern what it is. It's up to us to trust the process.

ROUND FOUR:
Death Wish

Weeks went by without Tippy touching me since the basement incident. I was hoping and praying that I wasn't his type or that he had forgotten all about me. I started thanking God for allowing me to go untouched. Unfortunately, I rejoiced too soon.

One night, as I lay in bed, I fell into a deep sleep. I could feel a presence in the room with me. I woke up. In the dim light, I could see the silhouette of a dark shadowy figure peering down at me from the edge of the bed. I shared the bottom bunk bed with my youngest sister while my older brother slept at the top. I knew that it was nobody but horny-ass Tippy. He climbed into the bed with me and started spooning me. I believed my baby sister was aware of what was going on. Next, Tippy's hands groped at my private parts. Soon, his fingers found their way into my undergarments, and he continued exploring.

"Oh God, not again," I thought. "Why is he here? Why is he hurting me like this?" Suddenly I heard footsteps in the hallway. Tippy's body stiffened. He moved his hands quickly and acted like he was asleep. My mom stepped inside the room. I was so relieved.

"Tippy," she said, slightly shaking him. "What are you doing in here?"

He rubbed his eyes like he was awakening from a deep sleep.

"Oh, I must've fallen asleep. I was reading the little ones a bedtime story," Tippy lied. Tippy stood and followed mom out of the room.

I was ashamed to show my face the next day. My body--my sacred temple, had been defiled by a robber and thief. I wanted to tell my mother what Tippy had done the night before, but I had learned my lesson when he pulled a shotgun on me. Exposure might cost all our lives. I decided against it since doing so the last time got me nowhere.

We were all invited to a Barbeque by my mother and Tippy's friends the following weekend. At the cookout, mom was drinking a lot, as usual. After making it home, we started watching television in the living room. Mom passed out on the couch. Tippy helped her into the bedroom. Afterward, he instructed us to go to bed as he sat on the sofa. When I stood, Tippy told me to stay behind. My stomach churned.

"I need to chat with you about something," he said.

I knew he was a bald-faced liar. He didn't want to do any talking.

That night, I was ready. I decided the next time he laid a finger on me would unleash my wrath. He would get the fight of his life. One of us was going to die that night. I was okay if it was me. At least I wasn't going out without a fight. I wasn't afraid of him for the first time in my life. I felt bold, like a lion.

I kept walking as if he didn't say a word,

He repeated himself, more forceful this time. "I said come here!"

I whirled around and glared at him. "No. I'm not coming. I'm not afraid of you," I said and stomped off.

His face transformed in an instant as he leaped from his seat.

Within a split second, he dived toward me. I ran into his and mom's bedroom screaming, trying my best to awaken mom. She didn't budge. She was too intoxicated. He grabbed me by the hair and dragged me into the dining room. Once there, he began pounding me in the face with his fist. One by one, they came with force. I realized then that I had to fight for my life. I screamed for mom, but she didn't come. No one was there to protect me.

As I broke free from his grasp, Tippy grabbed a wooden broom lodged by the trash can and whacked me across the face. It broke in half. I tumbled to the floor. As if that wasn't enough, he grabbed my head and flung it against the dining room window. Glass shattered everywhere. In that instant, my life flashed before my eyes. I knew that I was going to die. I had accepted my fate. I heard my sisters and brothers wailing in the distance, but the room was spinning and growing darker by the minute. An eerie calm washed over me. I felt like I was finally about to get my death wish.

"I can finally be free from this hell," I thought. I just hoped that God would protect my family while I was gone. Suddenly, I heard my mother screaming hysterically.

"What have you done? Why have you hurt my child this way!?"

That's all I remembered before passing out.

I woke up the following morning; I hadn't died after all. I was still lying on the dining room floor. Mom was standing over me, shaking me.

"I can't take her like this," I heard her rationalizing with Tippy. Look at her face! The state will take her away from us." They were debating on whether or not to take me to the hospital.

My entire body ached in pain; my face and eyes were swole. The swelling made it difficult for me to see clearly. I could not cry. There were no tears left. I brewed with anger and hatred. I was numb to any empathy for Tippy. I wanted him dead.

Nothing made sense to me about why this was happening to my family. What exactly did we do wrong? What exactly was our sin? My mother took us to church on Sundays, and I knew that God was real, so why was this happening? Was I destined for a life of suffering? Not having answers infuriated me. I was so tired of being Tippy's sex slave. Every time he ravished my body, a piece of me died.

Two months later, I began menstruating. I couldn't have been happier. I hoped Tippy wouldn't touch me for at least a week or two. I longed for my monthly cycle every month for this reason. Sadly, it would place my siblings in greater danger. All I could do was pray for them.

Due to the frequent commotion in our house, the neighbors started asking questions and snooping around. That made Tippy uneasy, so off we were moving again. I was so tired of being uprooted for the umpteenth time. New schools, new friends, new neighbors—it was all just too much for any child to go through. As usual, we re-enrolled at our new schools. Life went on as usual. I wondered how long before our next move.

One day mom forgot to pack my lunch, so she asked me to come back home during lunchtime. At that time, children were allowed to do so. My pulse raced; my palms sweated, and my stomach churned as I got closer to the house. I knew something was not right. Just as I suspected, Tippy answered the door. I immediately stopped in my tracks.

"Get your ass in here and hurry up," he commanded.

I reluctantly obeyed.

As soon as he closed the door, Tippy said, "Go upstairs and get naked."

After doing so, he didn't waste any time roaming my body freely as if it belonged to him. My skin crawled at the thought of him touching me and rubbing his body against mine. I couldn't bear to think about it any longer. I tried hard to focus on anything but what he was doing to my body.

ROUND FIVE:
Hidden in Plane Sight

After having sex with me, he ordered me to wash myself up and return to school. As I walked back, the image of him caressing me kept resurfacing. The closer I got to the school, the louder a voice in my head told me to keep going. I did just that. I didn't think about where I was going. I just kept walking. I realized that the only way I would escape Tippy's abuse was to free myself. No one else was coming to my rescue fast enough. I sincerely believed that once I got on my feet and found a place to live, I would return home to my mother and siblings. I intended to rescue everyone from the monster that had plagued our lives. That was my plan anyways.

I walked as far as I could to the nearest hospital, about a mile away. I entered the emergency room of Henry Ford Hospital, the main hospital in Detroit. I figured it would be a safe place to hang out until I figured out my next move. Besides, I needed a warm place to stay because the weather was colder. I entered the building and walked over to a nearby snack machine. I had three dollars on me. I purchased some chips and a can of soda. I found a seat in the lobby and ate my snacks. I entertained myself by watching people come in and out the door.

Hours went by. To my amazement, no one noticed me or questioned why I was there. I might as well have been invisible. I found a comfortable place to sleep in the emergency waiting area. I finally had a good night's sleep since I didn't have to worry about Tippy sneaking into my room and groping me. The hours turned into days. Throughout the day, I walked up and down the hospital corridors and visited the gift shop until everything closed. Afterward, I returned to the emergency waiting room area.

On the third night, I sat there watching tv as usual when the news came on. An image of my mother materialized on the screen. I sat erect in my chair as my heart began to pound in my chest. My mother was crying uncontrollably, asking for any information about my whereabouts. A picture of me flashed across the screen. A few of the people in the room glanced in my direction. I became nervous as their eyes side-watched me suspiciously. Many white folks thought blacks looked alike, I assumed. I should be fine.

Seeing my mom bawling her eyes out on tv saddened me deeply. It felt as if my heart shattered into millions of little pieces. I knew she must be going insane, wondering where I was and if I was safe. I toyed with the idea of returning home, but the problem was I didn't know if anything would change. I shuddered at the thought of what Tippy would do to me if I confessed to mom the real reason I had run away. I shuddered at the thought. I decided to take my chances anyway and return home for mom sake. I wanted her to know that I was alive and well. Besides, I was missing her too.

I got up and went outside. The cool evening air caused loose strands of hair to fly in my face. A few pieces got stuck in my mouth. I spat it out just as I spotted a cab. I flagged it down and gave the driver my home address. I sat in the back, wrestling with my decision. The closer I got to the house, the more I pondered telling mom the truth. I couldn't fathom being back under the same roof as the rapist who had just forced me to have sex with him only a few days earlier.

When we drew closer to my home, I spotted a large group of people littering our lawn, including a local news crew. I hardly recognized any of the faces. Cars were lined up and down our block and in our driveway. At that moment, I felt special. I was overwhelmed that they were all there to help my mom find me and to offer support for our family.

I got out of the cab and shut the door behind me. My mother's face lit up when she saw me. The crowd turned to follow her gaze. She ran over and embraced me, landing kisses all over my face. My siblings soon joined her side. They were all genuinely happy to see me. I was overwhelmed by the amount of love that my family was showing for me. They cared if I was dead or alive. And then there was Tippy's lying ass standing nearby like he was happy to see me. I'm sure he was, but for the wrong reasons.

My happiness was short-lived. Daunting questions began to harass my mind. "If all these people cared so much, why isn't anyone asking the right questions? Why aren't they digging deeper to see that all clues pointed to Tippy?" "Did they discover the dirty little secrets that were going on in our home? Did they care to know why I left? If they knew, would they put a stop to it?" I wondered. I guess I had to find out for myself. After strangers came by and wished me well, they began to disperse. After only a few people remained, mom and Tippy ushered me into the house and their room. Mom took a seat on the bed. Tippy and I remained standing.

Mom was the first to break the silence.

"Why did you leave, baby?" she asked tears in her eyes. "What is so bad that would make you want to run away? I was reluctant to answer, but the truth began to flow like water. I couldn't stop it from spilling out. I told mom how Tippy was at home when I had come from school and how he forced me to have sex with him. I explained how he threatened me if I said anything. I confessed that I stayed at the hospital and that her crying on television, concerned about my whereabouts, was my reason for coming home.

"I didn't do any such thing! I would never hurt her. I love all of you

38

unconditionally," Tippy lied through his vile teeth, trying his best not to raise his voice and risk someone overhearing him. I was appalled at how well he could lie.

"We'll continue this later," he hissed, storming out of the room.

Mom sat there blankly for a few minutes. Without uttering a word, she rose from the edge of the bed and walked out of the room. The front door opened and closed.

I told the truth again, but it had gotten me nowhere. I was heartbroken. With tears streaming down my face, I exited their bedroom and walked into mine. I stretched out across the bed with my shoes and clothes on. I heard voices outside my window. Mom and Tippy were seeing the remaining bystanders off. I lay there staring up at the ceiling until I dozed off. I awakened to mom tucking me under the covers and kissing my forehead. She had removed my shoes and clothing. I was only wearing my slip.

I had no way of knowing whether mom believed me or believed Tippy. She didn't utter a word about what I had told her. I hoped and prayed there wouldn't be any repercussions for what I had disclosed to mom. I was not in the mood for any drama. I wanted to enjoy the first night back, sleeping in my bed instead of cramped up in hospital chairs.

Weeks went by without Tippy laying a finger on me. I almost believed he had changed. I hoped that running away had scared him enough to get his shit together. As usual, that dream was short-lived. Out of the blue, he announced we would be moving again. That wasn't a good sign at all. I knew he was about to restart his wickedness. I made up my mind if he dared touch me, I would run away again.

After we had moved, he resumed his late-night molestations, plundering from room to room what didn't belong to him. I kept my promise to myself. The next day, I fled away from home. By now, I was 12 years old. I would run away again and again if I had to.

This time I stayed gone for over a week. I stayed in abandoned homes or anywhere else I could find to sleep. I was hungry and searching for a new place to sleep when I ran into a guy who offered to help me. He said I could stay with him. I was naïve, so I followed him. We spent the night in his car. The next day, I knew I had to get away from him. He drove me downtown. The first opportunity I got, I bolted from the car and ran into a clothing store. I crouched in a dressing room and hid until he left. I spotted him looking for me. I dared not come out until he was gone. He finally gave up his search and left. I came out to be sure. His car was nowhere in sight.

I wandered downtown until the shops closed for the remainder of the day. Hours passed. I noticed a street sign that read, "West Grand Blvd."

Next, I spotted a middle-aged man. Our eyes locked. "Hey, are you lost? Do you need help" he shouted across the street towards me.

"Yes," I admitted. By now, I was famished.

"My name is John," he said, walking over to where I was. "Follow me. I live right over there," he said, pointing towards a brick house not far away.

We both walked in the direction that he had pointed. When we arrived at his place, he opened the door and stepped inside. I followed behind him. The smell of cigars and Pine Sol filled the air. We were standing inside his kitchen. Not a single dish was in the sink.

"Would you like something to eat?"

"Sure," I said.

"Have a seat," he said, motioning for me to sit at the table. He opened the fridge, took out some Peanut Butter and Jelly, and plopped them down on the table. Next, he grabbed a butter knife and saucer from the dish rack and handed them to me. Afterward, he opened a cabinet, pulled out a half loaf of bread, and sat it in front of me. As I fixed a sandwich, he stepped out of the room, disappearing into an adjacent room.

Thirty minutes hadn't passed before knocking was heard at the door. It was mom and Tippy. I didn't have a clue how John knew how to reach them. They probably had been showcasing my picture on the news again. I could see the pain in mom's eyes as she and Tippy stepped inside. She was so broken. Tippy glared at me with pure hatred. I knew things were going to turn ugly when I got home. After small talk, they thanked John; I followed them to the car.

There was no warm homecoming this time around. As soon as I walked into the house, Tippy began beating me. I took the beating like a boss. It was the most brutal attack of my life. If he continued to touch me inappropriately, I would run away again.

That night, Tippy came into my room and threatened to kill my mother and everyone else in the house if I tried to leave again. I knew he was capable of doing such a thing. The look on his face confirmed his viciousness. I had to come up with an alternate plan to save my family.

ROUND SIX:
No Tears Here

The days inched on. The situation at home started getting worse. For no apparent reason, Tippy started beating mom daily when he got home from work. He became more violent with Venus too. I often watched in horror as mom got kicked in the back and stomach for the heck of it. If she tried to intervene, he would slap her around. Killing him was in my thoughts every day. When I thought about it, I could not stop. It was hard to turn off. All I had to do was wait for him to fall asleep and stab him in the chest with the kitchen knife. He would never hurt anybody else ever again.

"Why is this happening to us? Why won't you make him stop hurting us?" I continued questioning God. Every day, from the moment I opened my eyes until it was time to sleep, I conversed with GOD. I needed answers soon. I assumed I wasn't praying hard enough, so I prayed more fervently. Still, there was silence. By now, tears were frequently part of my existence. Crying was the only way I could find some relief from my psychological pain. I hoped that my tears would move God to act on behalf of my family. Until then, I would have to wait.

I prayed the same prayer over and over again for years to come. I wanted our nightmare to end, but it seemed almost hopeless. I wished it was all a bad dream. Of course, it wasn't; The monster I faced every day was just as real as they came.

It was 1978. Tippy continued to jump on mom as usual. One time I recall him using a jackhammer as his weapon of choice. I was so afraid that he was going to kill her. Her face was covered in blood and was starting to swell. That was the final straw for me. I planned on killing him that night. Since he wanted to act like an animal, I was going to slaughter him like one. I took mom's butcher knife and hid it to carry out my plan. Out of fear, Tina and Will ran out the back door to get help. They knew that I was serious about killing Tippy. They could see it in my eyes. Our neighbor Mr. John came over with his gun.

"Go to the house," he said to the rest of us kids. We obeyed. His wife Emma had the porch light turned on. As soon as we made it to the door, she let us in and quickly locked the door behind us. We ended up spending the night at our neighbor's house. Each of us was restless. We tossed and turned until daybreak.

The next morning after awakening, we peered out the window over to our house. Our car wasn't in the driveway, but an unfamiliar one was there. We hoped Tippy was gone. Each of us ran home, trying to sneak and get our clothes. We opened the door and rushed inside. Tippy was nowhere around. I asked mom where he was. She informed us he had left for the store. We then greeted Mrs. Turner and her kids, Tony and Rickey. They were sitting down on the couch. They had come because they were concerned that we hadn't been to school recently. While inquiring, a vehicle pulled up in the driveway. I glanced out the curtain; it was Tippy. There was nowhere to hide. Hopefully, he wouldn't try to fight while we had company was over. Tippy opened the door and stepped inside. His ice-cold glare scanned the room. Without a word, he walked over to the phone, picked up the receiver, and started dialing. It was the police. We listened in bewilderment as he made bogus claims that we had broken into his house.

When the police arrived, Tippy continued his accusation that we had broken into the house. No one could have anticipated what happened next.

"He's been raping these girls!" Mrs. Turner confessed to the police officers.

The entire room became quiet. The words seemed to reverberate off the walls.

The police officers turned toward Me, Venus, and Tina. "Is this true?"

Too ashamed to look up at the officers, we all admitted that it was.

In a blink of an eye, the officers handcuffed Tippy and read him his rights. We were all asked to come to the police station to give our statements. Once there, we were all interrogated and screened by female Sex Crime Unit officers and social workers. They asked us lots of questions separately that were both embarrassing and nerve-wracking because we feared they would take us from our mother. I was 13. Venus was about to turn 17. Our younger sister Claudia denied the allegations of being sexually assaulted by Tippy. Years later, she confessed to us that he had been molesting her since she was 6. Fear had caused her to block the trauma. About eight months before the court case, we moved again. This time it was four houses down.

When the trial started, the case turned brutal quickly. My siblings and I had to testify separately to ensure we didn't fabricate our story. There were four separate court cases. When it was my time to testify, I was embarrassed and ashamed. I felt like people were judging my momma and me. I feared that they would try to take us from her. My brother Will and I testified together.

A lot of Tippy's dark deeds finally got dragged out in the open, in the light where everyone could see what he had been hiding. Everyone was able to see that he was a monster. The testimonies that came forward were surreal. We discovered that Tippy was sleeping with his oldest daughter's husband and his sister Johnny. That explained why she always looked fearful when we came around. She knew what he was capable of and feared for our safety.

Two of his daughters testified. It turns out that he had been raping them as well. His first wife had accused him years prior, but it fell on deaf ears. Nothing stopped his quest for young flesh. Years earlier, I recalled seeing him jump on his oldest daughter. She was drunk, yet he beat her in the middle of the street. She accused him of raping her. Her testimony revealed she had been telling the truth. A few years later, she passed away due to health complications. During the trial, his youngest daughter died due to sickle cell disease. Her testimony yet was used as evidence.

Of course, being the liar that he was, Tippy denied everything. He said we were on drugs, had boys in and out of the house, and our eldest sister tried hitting on him. His family hated us for making those allegations against Tippy. Shucks, his daughters had accused him of the same things we had. I guess they were too blind to see the truth even when it was staring at them in their faces. His brother, our Uncle Booty, was vicious toward us. He was part Haitian and part Creo. His stare alone could chill the blood. To this day, Tippy's brother and relatives never forgave us.

In 1979, the jury ruled in our favor. Tippy got convicted on all four counts of sexual assault and battery. For raping Venus and Tina for years, he got Life in prison. For assaulting mom, Tippy got Life. For Will and me, he got 20-40 years. He would never see freedom again.

"It's yawls fault that my brother is in jail!" Uncle Booty hurled at our family in his thick Creo accent. I will never forgive yawl."

We were sorrowful that our truth angered him and divided our families, but as long as our nightmare had ended with our boogie man

45

never getting out of jail again, it was alright with us. There were no tears here.

Our younger brothers Tamar was four and DeAndre was three when their dad was convicted and imprisoned. Thankfully, both only vaguely remember what happened. We tried to protect them from finding out everything. The same rang true for all of us older siblings. We also tried to protect one another from being harmed by Tippy's demonic ass. It didn't do much good for us. Tippy yet found a way to get what he wanted when he wanted it. Tamar looks just like his dad and is yet in contact with his side of the family. DeAndre desired to visit him in prison to seek answers. He never did. He doesn't communicate with his father's family now. Years later, Tippy died in Jackson State Penitentiary in Detroit.

Mom's suffering didn't end after Tippy went to prison. Her health deteriorated. The severity of the beatings she suffered damaged her left eye. Surgery removed it. She continued drinking as if trying to drown out her mental anguish in the bottle. Years later, she developed throat cancer. Her vocal cord and half of her tongue were removed and replaced by a tracheostomy.

Her guilty conscience convinced her that she deserved cancer for not protecting us. We tried to make her see that she was doing the best she could and that it was not her fault that Tippy was a corruptible seed. There was no way that she could've known that he would treat us like he did. I don't think she ever forgave herself.

After the Tippy horror, Mom tried to put the pieces of her life back together. She gathered the courage to keep on living and loving. In the process, she got into another relationship with a man named Mr. Leonard.

After she and Mr. Leonard split, he developed cancer. I often visited him until he disclosed that he was attracted to me. I immediately stopped. A year later, after his diagnosis, he died. In the meantime, mom's cancer spread. Her lungs became infected, and she had to have one of them removed. Thanks to a slew of therapies and plenty of prayers, her cancer went into remission. For the first time in eleven years, mom was cancer-free.

Around 1980 or 1983, kids in the neighborhood began referring to our house as the "Kool-Aid house." We received food stamps because mom couldn't work. Everyone loved her cooking. She gave and did a lot for others around the community. Mom would give her last to ensure no one she knew was hungry or lacking anything. Although we didn't have much, she went without so we could have.

For years after Tippy's incarceration, I awakened between 3 and 4 a.m. every night in a cold sweat. My heart pounded against my chest as I gasped for air. I could smell Tippy's odor all around me as if he had been in the room. It seemed real. I knew mentally he was locked up and couldn't continue hurting me, but my body didn't know. Due to experiencing frequent trauma, my body stayed ready to fight, flee, or freeze. Survival was its highest priority. It couldn't discern between the real and the unreal. It continued responding the same as if the threat was real.

I was baffled by how childhood trauma would affect me even in adulthood. My past was stalking me. I didn't know when it would stop haunting me. How long would the agony last? Was there anything I could do to move forward? I had no option but to survive. Was this a battle with my demons or something else?

From a young age, I believed the negative words spoken about me. Some said I wouldn't ever succeed or amount to anything in life. My belief in their words became a self-fulfilling prophecy. I grew up with poor self-esteem and self-worth. I concluded that I was nothing more than a piece of trash. Not only did people treat me like trash, but I was used and then tossed aside like it.

I was often very depressed. I felt like an outsider. Even when I became an adult, this was the case. It seemed that my life was doomed for failure before it even began. I was out for the count in the ring of life. I lived in constant fear that tortured my young mind and robbed it of its innocence. I wandered around for years in the never-ending tunnel of hardships and setbacks. I barely existed. I was void of affection for life and true happiness. As a thirteen-year-old, I did not give a damn about anything involving me.

`Sometimes it didn't feel like my family cared about me, even though, deep down, I knew they did. The constant feeling of "not enoughness" (not good enough, not loved enough, not pretty enough, etc.) constantly led me into deviant behaviors, and I found myself doing things I never thought I would. For instance, I would sell my body for a few dollars to the highest bidder. It gave me a false sense of power. I also lied about my age to hook up with older guys. I was willing to share a bed with both men and women for some cash or a pack of cigarettes. I lost track of the number of sexual partners. Being promiscuous was the only way I could obtain the love I craved. All I needed to hear was how much they loved or cared for me; it temporarily filled the void in my heart. I didn't realize that I was only craving unconditional love and acceptance. I felt like a useless prostitute. I was so embarrassed about the person that I had become. My self-identity shattered. I would do anything to feel whole again.

Sometimes after mom paid the rent, I would sleep with the landlord to get it back. I would then put the money in her handbag. After she found it, I would convince her that it was money she may

48

have misplaced and should keep it for herself. After witnessing her sheer joy from being able to splurge with the extra cash, I temporarily felt good about myself. It didn't last long because I was doing grown-up things I had no business doing. I also was ashamed of stealing money from the elderly and other unthinkable things.

Some parents kept their children away from me. They were suspicious of my behavior and didn't want me to corrupt their kid's good behaviors with my tainted ones. I didn't blame them one bit. Little did they know, my mother's boyfriend conditioned me to whore around.

I started using marijuana and other drugs to dull the anguish I was experiencing daily. I snuck out of the house at night to avoid going to school. I got into fights, robbed the local corner store, and ran with the wrong crowd.

I was spiraling out of control fast, headed for destruction. If I didn't find help soon, I wasn't sure how much longer I would be alive. I was a lost, tainted, and fractured soul. It would take an act of God to make me whole again.

In 2008 my dad passed away from prostate cancer. Two years later, on November 12th, Mom eventually succumbed to her illness after a long and selfless life. Dad's urn went into her casket beside her body.

The years passed. I was now an adult with children of my own. I had my daughter Andrea when I was only 14 years old. Her dad was 27 years old. At 18, I gave birth to my son Mark. By the age of 22, I had twins named Lorraine and Fred. Their father was 15 years older than me.

FINAL ROUND:
THE REMEDY

School had always been my place of refuge. In high school, I was a straight-A student. In my early twenties, I worked and went to college. My preferred subject was mathematics. At the time, I was raising five-year-old twins and a nine-year-old son. My daughter Andrea was 13 years old. It became overwhelming, so I initially dropped out. The urge to complete empowered me to go back. I returned and finally finished. I felt like a rock star when graduation day arrived. I walked across the stage with my head held high. It was the first time that I had accomplished something meaningful to me on my own. I earned a degree in Accounting and an Associate Degree in Management. The feeling was surreal. I was around 27 years old.

When I first met Bobby, the father of the twins, my oldest daughter Andrea was 7. I was madly in love with him, but like me, he was battling his demons–alcoholism. It was not easy putting up with him, but he was always there for me when I needed him most. He started dabbling with crack cocaine and became addicted to that as well. Despite his addictions, he was still involved in his children's lives and kept an eye on them. He tried to get clean, but relapsed after his eldest son (14 years old, born by his wife), was convicted of murder and sentenced to life in prison. When our relationship finally ended, I pledged to myself that I would never enter into another one.

Unfortunately, I broke that promise. I met my first husband, Art, who I thought would be my forever love. He wasn't. He only left me even more psychologically wrecked than before. I was in a dark place in my life, so we separated.

In May 2002, I decided to finally go through with my suicide plan to rid myself of constant psychological pain. I remember the day vividly like it was yesterday. The kids were home, playing in the yard. My oldest daughter was in the kitchen cooking. Sinister voices from hell edged me on.

"Go ahead. Kill yourself. You can do it," the voices cackled.

As if in a trance, I walked outside to grab a can of gasoline. Afterward, I walked back into the house and up the stairs to my bedroom. I called Art to come over so that we could talk. I wanted him to witness me ending my life. When he arrived, I called him upstairs to my bedroom. We had only talked for about five minutes before I opened the gasoline bottle and began pouring the liquid all over my body.

"Look at what you made me do!" I spat at him.

Speechless, Art looked on in horror.

Next, I took a lighter and sat myself ablaze. I don't recall anything after that. I didn't feel anything while burning alive.

I awakened in the hospital. The skin was hanging from my arms, chest, and stomach. The taste of gasoline was in my mouth. My hair was gone; my eyes singed. Yet, God spared my life again. My process of recovery was gruesome. Instead of checking on me, Art stole items out of the house. I assume to finance his drug habit. I eventually moved on with my life.

I remained single for years afterward, keeping my promise of celibacy. I wanted to focus on healing myself physically, mentally, and spiritually. A man was the farthest thing on my mind. As the saying goes, "when you aren't looking for a blessing, that's when God usually gives you one."

When I worked at CVS, I met a guy named Jeffrey. His demeanor was always warm and welcoming whenever he came into the store. I had no desire to learn more about him, but he made it obvious he was interested in me. Even though I gave him the cold shoulder, it didn't stop him from trying to conversate. Jeffrey had no problem telling me about himself. I learned that he had recently relocated from Chicago. He usually went to Walmart and hung out there when he got off work at 5:30 am. That changed after COVID-19 struck.

Sometimes during the wee hours of the morning, it was hard to keep my eyes open. Jeffrey's chit-chat helped me to stay awake. His persistence and attentiveness paid off. Our casual conversations evolved into a friendship. Often he waited until 8:00 a.m. for me to finish my shift, although he had already worked a 12-hour shift.

When I did get off, instead of driving straight home, he and I would sit in my car and talk for hours while listening to R&B classics in the background. I discovered that we both enjoyed the same kinds of music. Our conversations helped us to learn a lot about one another. Most of the time, it was after 10 a.m. when we decided to part ways.

Even though we had a lot in common, I was careful not to let my guard down too quickly. I was open and honest that I wasn't interested in a sexual relationship with him. I would only be intimate with my future husband if it were God's will for me to get married. Then and only then would that man be able to get the goods. Jeffrey wasn't phased at all by my bluntness. He assured me that he was there for the long haul. He agreed to embark on the journey of celibacy with me. Neither of us wanted sex to be the focus of our budding relationship. At times we both were tested. Yet no matter how difficult it was to remain faithful to our decision, we persevered. Jeffrey was patient and committed to the process, always respecting my wishes.

Jeffrey had so many positive qualities that I admired. He was a decent human being in every way. In addition to his ability to make me laugh regularly, his devotion to family inspired me. Besides his loving stepfather, whom he and his brother call dad, Jeffrey has strong women (his mother and aunts) impacting his life. He cares a lot about them, and it shows. As a result, Jeffrey learned to treat all women–especially black queens, with respect and compassion. He treated me the same way whenever I was with him. I always felt special. He always provided for my needs.

We communicated for months before finally letting down our defenses and becoming vulnerable with each other. Jeffrey was reluctant for me to come to visit his home. It took a long time before I was allowed to enter. One day after our early morning car talks, I followed him home to find out where he lived.

"Can I come in?" I asked.

"I don't think that's a good idea," he said. "We both might get weak," he teased.

"We're both grown," I said.

I could tell by his fidgeting that there had to be another reason he didn't want me to come in. I continued to probe. I needed to know what kind of man I was dealing with for my safety.

He finally gave in and told me the truth. "The place is a wreck. There is so much to fix. I feel humiliated," he admitted. He turned away from my gaze. The look of distress on his face convinced me not to press the topic further.

Days later, I finally convinced him to let me enter his home. I immediately saw why he was so hesitant. The place was full of clutter and debris--a typical bachelor's pad. It needed a thorough cleaning.

Upon further investigation, I discovered I was the first woman he had ever permitted to enter his living quarters. My feminine instincts took over, and I started cleaning his entire apartment. I wanted to be able to sit comfortably.

After seeing my finished product, Jeffrey's face beamed with delight.

"Wow, you have a gift for aesthetics!" he practically squealed. You have a knack for making things fit together perfectly."

I felt pleased that he thought well of my efforts.

I permitted him to meet my children a few days later. They were all instantly in love with him. I valued what they had to say. Their likes or dislikes were my way of determining whether or not to keep him as a friend.

As our friendship started blossoming, I received a phone call informing me that my oldest son had suffered a seizure in Detroit, Michigan, where he lived. I had to take a two-and-a-half-week leave of absence from work. As soon as I finished packing, I headed out of state to be with him. When I arrived at the hospital where he was, the doctors gave me the diagnosis. My son had Cancer and a brain tumor that needed removal.

Every day Jeffrey encouraged me and checked on the status of my son. He made sure I knew he missed me.

"Whenever you're ready, come back to Little Rock. I will be here awaiting your return," Jeffrey reassured.

He then provided gas money to get me back and forth from Detroit to Arkansas. I grew even more attached to Jeffrey during those trying times. My emotions were all over the place. I found him to be a fantastic source of comfort. I had no clue that I would end up falling for him hard, that he would sweep me off my feet, and that one day, he would become my husband. Well, that's what happened, and in that order.

A few months later, Jeffrey proposed to me. I said "Yes," without hesitation.

Looking back on our courtship, Jeffrey alleges that I flirted with him first and asked him to marry me.

"You always held your head high and back arched as you sashayed in front of me," he teased. "I believe you knew what you were doing. Well, it worked. You caught my attention."

"You know that you were digging me first," I rebutted.

Who dug who first has become a little joke between us.

My faith in God had brought me to my Boaz. The beauty of our wedding was not due to the ceremony's elaborate decor but rather to the abundance of love, joy, and peace that enveloped the room. I believe God gave Jeffrey to me as a reward for enduring all I had gone through.

He is my custom gift from God. We complement one another like pieces in a puzzle. We both prioritize God and our families above everything else. We are open and honest with each other and pray a lot. Before we go to bed, we quote the following scripture almost every day:

"In your anger do not sin: Do not let the sun go down while you are still angry, and do not give the devil a foothold" (Ephesians 4:26-27).

Before leaving the house, we usually quote our favorite scripture "Truly I tell you, whatever you bind on earth will be bound in heaven, and whatever you lose on earth will be loosed in heaven." If we are in a rush or forget, we must do our morning text no matter what.

"Again, truly I tell you that if two of you on earth agree about anything they ask for, it will be done for them by my Father in heaven. For where two or three gathers in my name, there I am with them" (Matthew 18:18-20).

We say "later" instead of "goodbye." after warmly hugging each other. We are both aware that nothing is certain in this world. We have decided to savor every second we have. Our partnership is one of joy and harmony. Maintaining a relationship with God is a huge factor in our success as a couple.

One day before heading to work, Jeffrey pulled me close to him and planted a kiss on my forehead.

"You are such a blessing to me," he whispered. "You have a wonderful way of keeping me in check."

I looked up and returned the kiss fully on his lips. Despite all the blows that life had thrown me, I finally felt safe enough to retire my boxing gloves. There was more to life than just fighting and trying to survive. I inhaled and sunk into Jeffrey's strong protective arms allowing myself to surrender to his love. It felt good; He felt good. I had what I always wanted—unconditional love. With God and Jefferey, I had all the love that I needed.

Despite all the hell, my siblings and I turned out well. Venus, my oldest sister, became a licensed Evangelist and Missionary. She still lives in Detroit, not far from the church and house we grew up. Careerwise, Venus is a mortgage banker. She also served 11 years in the army fresh out of high school. Tina became a Missionary and a Pharmacist at Rite-Aid, where she has worked for over 40 years. My oldest brother, Will, became a church Elder and Pastor. He has been the head of a department at Dillard's for over 20 years in Tampa, Florida. DeAndre spent 22 years in the Marines. He retired and taught High School. He also has retired from there. Tamar went to prison for drugs and served 15 yrs. in federal prison, but he made mom a promise to get himself together. As an entrepreneur, he owned a mobile detail shop for 25 years. Claudia is a loss prevention supervisor/inspector for 60 stores in Michigan. As for me, I am currently an author, armor-bearer, and church intercessor. I believe God will continue to add to this list.

The End

ABOUT THE AUTHOR

After years of being burnt out by the typical gimmicks found at most churches, Charlotte and Jeffrey Hill found a church they both could call home. She is active in ministry and serves as her pastor's armor-bearer. Mr. Hill worships alongside her. Their church has become a safe place for Charlotte to go through deliverance, heal, and rediscover herself. She is taking life one day at a time and facing issues through the power of prayer. She surrenders painful memories each time they surface. Mrs. Hill participates in a women's group called Mothers of Israel and Kingdom Recovery. Lastly, Charlotte enjoys spending time with her grand and great-grandbabies every chance she gets.